William Bence Jones

The Irish Church from the point of view of one of its layman

William Bence Jones

The Irish Church from the point of view of one of its layman

ISBN/EAN: 9783744741248

Printed in Europe, USA, Canada, Australia, Japan

Cover: Foto ©Lupo / pixelio.de

More available books at **www.hansebooks.com**

THE

IRISH CHURCH

FROM

THE POINT OF VIEW OF ONE OF ITS LAYMEN

BY

W. BENCE JONES, M.A. Oxon.

SECOND EDITION MUCH ENLARGED

LONDON

THOMAS BOSWORTH, 215 REGENT STREET

1868

NOTICE.

The First Edition of this Pamphlet was repeatedly referred to in the Debate in the House of Lords on the Irish Church, June 1868.

A few facts and figures that were stated in the First Edition, on the best authority then attainable, have been corrected from the Irish Church Commission Report and other sources. The alterations in no way affect the arguments.

LONDON: PRINTED BY
SPOTTISWOODE AND CO., NEW-STREET SQUARE
AND PARLIAMENT STREET

THE IRISH CHURCH

FROM THE POINT OF VIEW OF ONE OF ITS LAYMEN.

A GREAT MANY LAYMEN in the Irish Church, while recognising that its present *status* cannot be maintained, are deeply dissatisfied that it should be made the subject of party strife.

They know the weak points of their Church better than those to whom it is only a question of politics, because they know them from personal experience ; they think it however a question needing the most deliberate and careful judgment of the best minds, not only on account of its great intrinsic difficulties, but because it touches all concerned in their deepest feelings, and in the best (and worst) parts of their nature, and because there is great danger of real mischief being done by a mistaken course, in the increase of religious strife—Ireland's greatest curse.

No question ever suffered more by the way in which it was brought forward. All that was ever said against abstract resolutions applies with twofold force to the doings of last Session. The question is one about which it is very easy to form and express a general opinion, as was done clearly enough by the House of Commons more than thirty years ago, and yet, after years of struggle, that opinion was again let go, because of the difficulties in the practical details even of the small measure then contemplated. The difficulties are really in the details, and will not be fully seen till the attempt to draw a Bill is made. In the meantime men have been committing themselves to abstract assertions of all sorts in a way quite unusual upon a question of so much importance. Yet there are involved in it principles of right and wrong, upon which so far there has been no discussion at all— questions of the right to tithes as the original ecclesiastical endowment of Ireland ; the right to much property acquired by the Church since the Reformation ; the equitable rights of the whole body of the Church, as well as of individuals; rights of the laity, no less than of the clergy, that cannot be set aside on those principles of honest and fair dealing that have hitherto characterised the British Parliament. So vague has been the sketch of the plan in contemplation, that it has been understood in two opposite senses by those who advocate it. By some, as Mr. Coleridge, at Exeter, it has been stated as a plan to leave to the Church a bonâ fide three-fifths of its property. According to others, the three-fifths is a mere illusory calculation, that will benefit individual clergymen only, and strip the Church of almost everything.

Whatever is right to be done (and I am far from saying it is right much should not be done), surely this is not a question to be settled by a leap in the dark like that attempted last session. It is for the good of both Roman Catholics and Protestants, no less than of the whole nation, that the momentous interests concerned should be fully taken into account and settled on some large view of fairness to all, instead of for the gratification of religious ill-will or the party requirements of the day. The opposite of wrong is by no means always right. It may be true that the Established Church in Ireland is unjust, but it is easy in applying a remedy to commit a still greater injustice, and make the change, instead of a benefit, the source of worse mischief.

There is a preliminary point on which it is necessary men's minds should be made up before the main question is reached. Is the question to be settled for the good of Ireland and the contentment of her people, or to please English voluntaries and for their contentment?

It may seem a matter of course to say that the question is to be settled for the good of Ireland and the contentment of her people; but it is not so in fact.

No doubt in theory the motive for the proposed change is to conciliate Roman Catholics and to make them more contented. But the whole manner of the change, and the frequent declarations against any gain in a pecuniary sense to the Roman Catholic Church (however otherwise desirable or reasonable) out of the surplus ecclesiastical funds, which it is over and over again asserted are the property of the whole Irish people, is nothing less at best than, whilst granting a favour, to accompany it with so many insulting slaps in the face. The case of those who contend that the Anglican Church should continue as it is may be bad, but assuredly it is not half so bad or so absurd as the case of those who in one breath contend that the ecclesiastical endow-ments belong to the Irish people at large, and yet that the object in favour of which the great majority would wish to apply those endowments is on no account to have any share of them.

The answer of Liberals is, that Scotch Presbyterians and English Dissenters will resist any benefit to the Roman Catholic Church by money. But what is this but to say that the question is to be settled according to the likings of the Presbyterians and Dissenters and not for the good of Ireland ?

Anybody might suppose that money was the only source of strength ; that without money the Roman Catholic Church is harmless ; that its power of mischief is derived from the possession of money, and any other way of helping it is allowable.

If the question is not to be settled in the interest of Ireland, it would have been much better to let it alone. To raise it for the sake of the Irish Roman Catholics, and then settle it for the satisfaction of some one else, can never end in good. For the moment the loss to their old antagonist pleases the Roman Catholics, but it is as certain as anything can be, that if the settlement is not fairly in accordance with Roman Catholic interests, in a few years the subject will be seen in its true light, and will be a greater cause of discontent than it hitherto has been.

In the name of common sense, is it worth while to face an immense change of this sort, with all its difficulties and hardships and evils, running counter to the feelings of the great body of the members of the Anglican Church in these kingdoms, and for the satisfaction of some Presbyterians and Dissenters and extreme Protestants to do it in such a way as to fail to content the large majority of the Irish people? Whether the thing itself be right or wrong to be done may of course be disputed ; but admitting for the sake of argument that it is to be done, surely no man of sense and intelligence of whatever opinions political or religious can doubt, that it is for the good of the nation that it should be done in such a way as will best promote the peace of Ireland. The abstract prejudices of extreme Protestants and of Presbyterians and Dissenters have a claim to proper weight in their proper place, but ought not to be decisive of a great question of this sort, involving the permanent interests of the empire.

I think it is clear that if any such mode of settling the Irish Church question as was sketched last session is carried, it will unavoidably end in the mere secularisation of the endowments. They must be applied either to religious or secular uses. There is no middle sort of use. Those benevolent or practically beneficent uses that have been spoken of, as education, relief of the poor, hospitals, &c., are either religious or secular. The religious uses are open to just the same difficulties as applying the money to other more direct Roman Catholic purposes. The other sort of uses are just secularisation and nothing else. The

favourite idea seems to be, to apply the money to education, and use that now paid by Government for education
towards the promotion of railways, and for railway reform in
Ireland. But this in truth only raises the question, Which
thimble the pea is under? and the funds of the Irish Church
might just as well and more honestly be handed over to the
railways at once. The medical relief of the poor in Ireland is
admirably provided for already, including hospitals. Mere
relief of the poor would only relieve the land of poor rates,
unless given to those who do not now seek relief, which would
still further lessen their independence, already too small, and do
more harm than good. Additional free asylums for the aged
and infirm, which have been mentioned (I suppose it is meant for
persons not mere paupers), would be jobbed inevitably by every
one with a shadow of influence, even down to Poor Law
guardians, and do the same harm as unlimited Poor Law relief.
Public works in Ireland is only another name for private jobs,
and if any large sum each year had to be got rid of for such
purposes, it would cause an amount of jobbery such as the
nation has not seen before, and increased demoralisation. Lord
Russell thinks the question, What is to be done with the money?
can be very easily settled. As a resident, having spent thirty
years in improving an estate, and certainly being interested
keenly in every sort of improvement in the country, moral and
physical, I believe it is a question of overwhelming difficulty.
I cannot see the solution of it, and if it has to be decided now,
I believe it will long retard any settlement.

There is great and increasing objection in the minds of all
intelligent and educated men in Ireland, both Roman Catholics
and Protestants, to Secularisation in any form. It is not necessary to go into the disputed question of the origin of tithes ; but
thus far at least is certain, that there is neither proof nor probability of their having been in any sense the gift of the State.
All probability is in favour of the opinion that tithes were origi-
nally paid by private persons as a fulfilment of the duty of giving
of their substance to God's service. The measure of a tenth was
doubtless taken from the Mosaic law ; and the duty was strongly
urged by the clergy. When the practice had become common,
it may have been made compulsory on all by the State ; but
this was very different from the State itself giving the property.
In substance the gift was that of the private landowners, out of
whose lands it was paid. There must have been an earnest
and general feeling that the payment was one really for God's
sake, before the State could have made compulsory so heavy a
tax. It could not at first have been enforced on unwilling people.
There is, therefore, good ground for the feeling which weighs

so much with many right-minded men of all persuasions, that to secularise the tithes is nothing less than to Rob God. Granting even that there are good reasons for depriving the Irish Church of much of its revenues, why are the conscientious feelings of such men to be set at naught in the manner of doing it to gratify the Voluntaries and other extreme parties?

It is sometimes said that the 25 per cent. reduction when the tithe rent charge was made payable by the landlords instead of by the tenants was so much given to them, and was so a precedent of secularisation. But such was not really the case. When the rent charge was payable by the small and poor tenant, large sums were unavoidably lost, the costs of collecting it were very considerable, and difficulties and disputes of all kinds were continual, in some cases even ending in outrage and murder. If the rent charge had continued payable by the tenant till the time of the famine, it is certain that for years the clergyman would not have received anything. As it was, in hundreds of cases the landowner paid the clergyman his rent charge without a shilling of abatement, out of farms from which he himself received nothing at all;—over whole estates the clergyman did not lose anything, whilst the payment of his rent charge absorbed one-fourth, one-third, and even one-half, of the total receipts of the estate for years. Now he gets his payments from a few without any expense if he is a man of the least business capacity, and I believe the change has, on the whole, and on the average, given the clergy as large a net income as they would have had under the old system, and without trouble or risk.

It is not for me as an Anglican Churchman to advocate the endowment of the Roman Catholic Church. It is for Roman Catholics to act and speak for themselves. The declarations of the Roman Catholic bishops on this question not long ago, and the speeches of the Roman Catholic M.P.'s in the House of Commons—though there is reason to believe the M.P.'s went beyond the intention of the bishops, and the bishops having, from whatever motive, used the ambiguous phraseology so often adopted by them, now desire to restrict their words to a narrower meaning—were their own act and deed. It is evident that these declarations form a most curious contrast to the eagerness with which chaplaincies to gaols, workhouses, and all other public institutions are sought by the Roman Catholic clergy in Ireland, and the keenness with which the salaries of such chaplaincies are canvassed and fought for. Yet these chaplains are far more under the control of boards of laymen—many of whom are Protestants—than Parish Priests, drawing stipends, would be under the Government. Nor is this readiness to accept such paid chaplaincies confined to Ireland. We had the spectacle last session of the very same Roman Catholic members, who early in the session expressed the most virtuous objection to the payment of stipends to Roman Catholic clergymen in Ireland, urging that it should be made compulsory on the Protestant visiting justices to pay salaries to the Roman Catholic chaplains of gaols in England, though it is certain gaol chaplains are under a degree of active and efficient control by the Visiting justices and Home Secretary much more strict than that of their own Bishops, and quite beyond any control of the State that would be possible if the Roman Catholic parish clergy were endowed. Of course, it is easy to draw ingenious distinctions between the two cases. But in truth the principle is the same in both. The distinctions only turn on conditions and modes in which the stipends are payable. How deep the objection against stipends to the Roman Catholic clergy goes may be judged of accordingly.

But that which is put forward by most Liberals as the ground of attack against the Irish Church is the necessity for religious equality. The question however at once arises, Equality with what? and in what respects?

The strength of the case against the Irish Church in the minds of the educated classes in England is, that the religion of the majority in England is the established and endowed Church, and the religion of the majority in Scotland; whilst in Ireland it is the Church of the minority; the Church of the much larger majority there having no such advantages. Though the Establishment in Scotland has not a majority, yet the difference in doctrine between it and the Free Church is so small as still to leave it true that the *religion* of the majority is the endowed religion. It is the sense of these facts, that in these days when all are equal in Parliament, has produced that feeling among educated men of the Church arrangements in Ireland not being just, to which the present movement against the Irish Church is due.

If, however, the English Church and Kirk of Scotland are to remain as they are, it is giving credit to Irish Roman Catholics for very small acuteness to suppose that they will not see, that by the secularisation of the property of the Irish Church they are not placed in the same position as the majority in England and Scotland, or anything like it. It will be just the old story of Roman Catholic emancipation over again. For the moment, Roman Catholics will be pleased at the blow to their old rival, and any amount of statements and assurances that are wished for will be forthcoming; but all the time the more educated and thoughtful amongst them are openly saying that they do not join in these assurances. They wholly dissent from secularisation ; and when the excitement is over they will be listened to, and the mass of Roman Catholics will see that they have not attained equality, that the very principle upon which the party favourable to their claims based their right has not been carried out. All the former discontent will again arise, with this difference, that the antagonism will then be between the Roman Catholics and the English Government, instead of between the Roman Catholics and the Irish Church.

If any one wishes to know the feelings of educated Roman Catholic laymen, let him read the pamphlets of Mr. Aubrey de Vere. It is equally clear from the pamphlet of Dr. Moriarty, Roman Catholic bishop of Kerry, that one of the best of the Roman Catholic bishops holds the same views.

It sounds well to talk of the liberality of Roman Catholic flocks, and where the parish is rich and the Roman Catholic priest well paid, no doubt he wishes for no change ; but there are Roman Catholic clergymen in Connaught whose incomes are only £60 a year, and however it may suit the views of the majority of the Roman Catholic bishops and politicians to declare against the payment of stipends by the Government to the Roman Catholic clergy, it is the general belief of intelligent men in Ireland, in which I fully share, that the majority of the Parochial clergy wish for such payment on fair terms, and that the whole body of the lower orders of Roman Catholics, on whom the burden of paying their clergy now mainly falls, desire that payment above all things—a hundred times more than the removal of any abstract grievances of the Established Church.

I do not think these facts have been at all considered. Party interests have alone been taken into account—what would tell on the elections—not the permanent good of Ireland ; and the snap reply has been eagerly put forward, that the Roman Catholics do not wish for any part of the endowments, when the truth is not a sixpence has been ever offered them. The question, however, is one more for Roman Catholics than for Anglican churchmen. There is no doubt the prevailing opinion in England at this moment is adverse to Roman Catholic endowment, and I have only brought the subject prominently forward because I do not think it right to conceal my strong conviction of its immense importance. There is not the difficulty some suppose in machinery for the purpose. Power to a non-political Commissioner to make grants in aid of any Roman Catholic parish or religious object in it, on a memorial from any bishop or clergyman or twelve lay parishioners, asking for such grant and to such amount as the surplus funds disposable allow, would get over most objections. If no memorial was presented, of course the money would have to be otherwise applied.

Whenever the point has been started, it has been not discussed, but just hooted down. But it is one that will force itself into notice sooner or later. It is well to observe too, that the mischiefs arising out of the proposed disestablishment of the Irish Church, as a precedent to be used hereafter against the Church in England, are caused wholly by this. If the principle of equality was really acted upon in regard to the Roman Catholic Church in Ireland, and it was put on anything like the same footing as the Churches of England and Scotland in regard to endowment, the measure would be no precedent against those Churches hereafter.

Here I must make a digression. The existence of disaffection, and especially of Fenianism, is often put forward by men of the highest position as the reason for the movement against the Irish Church. There is great ignorance in England of the real state of things in Ireland. The whole social state in the two countries is so unlike, that facts in Ireland, especially when seen without the surrounding and often qualifying details, produce a different impression from the true one on English minds. Notably, facts relating to the worst parts of the country, and often only exceptional there, are thought to apply to the whole country and at all times.

With some too even of the highest in England, instead of that strong judgment that grasps the very substance of facts amid whatever exaggeration and colouring, and intuitively seizes on the whole truth, there seems to have grown up a habit of easy belief in the dressed-up untruths of any schemer, if his story only tells in favour of the party views of the day. Stories often merely sentimental, that any one used to weighing evidence can see owe their whole point to the colouring, and that rest on the authority of men who every one of character in Ireland, of whatever opinions, knows to be undeserving of credit, are believed without hesitation. Now, in no place on earth is the art of dressing-up for a purpose a story founded on a modicum of facts, or on no facts at all, so well understood as in Ireland. That want of truth which is the great fault of the Irish character, and the unscrupulousness arising therefrom, make such practices easy and common to an extent that cannot be believed possible in England. Sound common sense is therefore the first qualification for judging of any Irish question.

When the Fenian outrages at Manchester and Clerkenwell showed that there was ill-will on the part of some classes of Irishmen towards England, it seemed to take people there by surprise, as if it was something unexpected and greatly to be feared. Those, however, who knew Ireland, were quite familiar with this ill-will. It is no novelty. It has been there as long as any one can remember. It is just the legacy of the old troubled times, of centuries of lawlessness, and of half savagery half civilisation, and had its origin, as Mr. Goldwin Smith has so strikingly shown in his book on 'Irish History and Irish Character,' from the half-conquered state of the country. It has been kept alive by the differences between Celt and Saxon character, between Protestant and Roman Catholic, between landlord and tenant, by the envy of the poor and backward towards the rich and prosperous country. These centuries of lawlessness, and the backward social state caused thereby, are the key to all Irish questions. The improvement has been immense, but it began so late and from so low a point relatively to England, that men do not recognise how great the progress has been. It is easy to ignore these things, and attribute the evils to other causes, but it is this backward state of society from top to bottom, where no class is much better or worse than another, that is the root of the evil. When all equally need improvement progress is necessarily slow. Great as the change has been, long years will yet be required to reach generally a higher state.

Outrages have always been of the essence of Irish disaffection : to succeed in causing fear is its very life. There is something in the character of the people that makes intimidation the first thought in any dispute. If two boys fall out in the street, instead of stripping off their jackets and setting to, they will shout and threaten and scold at each other for half an hour, the one object being to frighten the enemy. It is the same with grown-up men, with politicians in Parliament as well as common people. Threats without a bit of bottom in them are the first and immediate resource on every occasion, and always with a deliberately purposed intention.

But in reality there is no backbone in the disaffection any more than in the threats. The men who take part in it, of whatever class, are not those who carry weight even with their own sort. They have not the character to give them influence among their fellows. They are full of vanity and boasting and jealousy of each other—an empty melodramatic display and desire to be thought greater than their neighbours is their leading characteristic. The acute intelligence of the people helps to keep them powerless. Nobody goes into anything of the kind without keeping one eye constantly fixed over his shoulder to secure a safe retreat ; and they see through one another's failings and schemings and want of truth thoroughly ; the result is, that no real trust in each other is possible.

On the other hand, they understand how to talk and act sedition and half sedition to perfection ; the scheme is drawn out and plans are arranged on paper as if the thing was a reality instead of an imposture. In a newspaper the one looks as well as the other, and the end of causing fear is attained. Nothing has done more mischief than the statements that have been often made in England of the danger of Fenianism and of Irish disaffection as a reason in favour of measures that have been proposed. Every such statement is a positive triumph to these men.

But this ill-will has gradually and greatly lessened as the country has advanced and become more prosperous. The masses of idle, half-employed people are no longer there. In large cities there is still a mischievous class, and in the small towns a limited number of scamps, but in very few country districts does the material for any dangerous movement exist. Every year the class of farmers in good circumstances and with much property to lose, in stock &c., is increasing, and year by year both in town and country every one who gets into trouble of any sort, personal or pecuniary, or caused by sedition, forthwith emigrates.

The classes actively sharing in disaffection now are quite different from those who formerly took part in it. So late as the days of repeal a large part of the Roman Catholic farmers and shopkeepers were in the agitation. These classes as a body were opposed to Fenianism—no class was so frightened at it as the farmers. The frequent remark was, 'What do they make a trouble for now; we were never before so well off?' The movement lay almost entirely among a low class of shop-boys and idle youngsters about towns. Any chance farmer's son who joined it was at once promoted to be an A. or B., or some such mysterious dignity, showing how few of the sort they had. Except in large towns and a few country districts, it was a mere game of brag of the most contemptible kind, whose main strength lay in the fears of the timid. It may be unwise to despise an enemy however weak. It is more unwise to overrate his strength when really contemptible.

It was no doubt right for the Government to take precautions, if only to save ignorant people from the effects of their own folly, and the much talked of suspension of the Habeas Corpus Act was necessary on account of the Americans, but really for them only. I can say, as one who went through the whole of it, with everything to lose and no possible protection, that in my judgment there never ought to have been any serious alarm in the minds of sensible men. Why then it will be asked was there fear in so many minds ? There are men still alive who can tell all about the events of 1798 and since, in their own neighbourhood, from what they saw as boys, and the memories of the horrible outrages on both sides are still fresh in men's minds from tradition. In 1822 this was noted by the Duke of Wellington (see Vol. ii. p. 597 of the Correspondence lately published) and it is true still. Numbers too are still alive who took part in repeal and later rebellious movements, though they have since settled down into sober enough citizens. So when the old song was heard, albeit set to another tune, and with very inferior performers, it was not hard to move the old feelings. Some were frightened by the former memories, and others, on the opposite side, joined in shouting applause, who all the time would not have endangered a finger or risked 5l. in the cause, and would even have helped to crush it, if they thought it had the least chance of success. It is forgotten that it takes, not years, but generations, to change the ideas and feelings of a people. Time is the only cure of grievances that arise much more from long past and sentimental wrongs, and from unreasonable expectations, than from existing or removable causes.

Unhappily our system of government by party fosters these unreasonable expectations. Proposals are made and encouraged that can never be carried out in the sense in which they are understood in Ireland. Knowledge and common sense on economical subjects are wholly wanting in Ireland ; and there is always the hope that in some political conjuncture a part at least of what is desired may be yielded. Politicians deliberately work these feelings among ignorant people for party and personal objects, and thus ill-will is kept alive to the infinite hurt of the country. I know of course how easy it is to give the sentimental answer to such statements as these. But sentiment will never make things sound that are unsound. Let the blame be where it may for what is past, the same sound principles that produce prosperity elsewhere can alone produce it in Ireland.

It must be borne in mind that nowhere in the world is the game of hunting with the hounds and running with the hare so well understood. Any movement like Fenianism, however weak, is seen at once to give a handle that can be turned to account for other objects, and it is forthwith worked, and the movement encouraged *up to a certain point* for those objects. Whilst Fenianism was active the Roman Catholic clergy and politicians, almost without exception, made light of it, and rightly in my judgment. Since then the leaders of the party have one day treated it as the gravest possible danger to England, and the next urged the immediate liberation of the culprits as guilty of no offence and the cause of no danger! This is the explanation of the immediate effect of decided measures of repression by the Government. So large a part of the movement is hollow, that the first squeeze causes it to collapse. This too is the meaning of the sympathy for the Manchester murderers, and of the never-ceasing efforts of many Irish politicians, and of part of the Irish press, to shield the Fenian culprits of all sorts, and all others guilty of sedition, from punishment. Fair dealing and a resolute hand together are all powerful in Ireland, but any one who trusts to fair dealing without the resolute hand is just delivering himself up for a prey. No doubt in the view that all discontent and misdoings of the people are caused by bad laws—as if men were not to blame for their own faults and sins, because they may have an excuse for them—these things have little weight. I wish those who thus account for Irish evils would try a seven years' residence and familiar dealing with the people. They would then be better judges of the source of the evils of the country, and their true extent. In truth, a familiar residence in Ireland for any man of common sense would prove a cure for a great many illusions. Since the day when the roaring Lion proved to be only Bottom the Weaver, never was there such a disproportion between the thing pretended and its reality. Modern journalism has, no doubt, on the whole great advantages, but it has also its mischiefs. One of these is the facility it gives for systematic and false colouring and twisting of everything great and small for a purpose that I have spoken of. The papers constantly recount most ferocious sentiments uttered by men who we on the spot know to be of very harmless dispositions, and occurrences the most commonplace are, by the suggestion of motives and suitable dressing, made to bear a meaning that by no means belongs to them, and we are believed to live in a state of hatred and enmity with neighbours with whom we get on, upon the whole, in much peace and comfort.

It is commonly believed that Roman Catholics and Protestants live in constant enmity in Ireland. Every extreme act and word of violent partisans on either side is taken as representing the feelings of the masses towards each other. I have little knowledge of the North, which is as different from the rest of Ireland as Ireland is different from England. But in the South, where, though the Protestants are in a decided minority yet there are many districts in which they number one in four or five, this mutual ill-will does not exist. Here and there individuals on both sides may be ready for strife, and where proselytism is attempted a feeling of ill-will is found; but the great majority of the people on both sides mix together in the ordinary relations of life as if no such difference existed. Honest men of one religion will be found trusting and helping honest men of the other without any distinction or hesitation. An election for Parliament or any local office will bring out

religious differences, and every rogue invariably tries to make
capital out of religion for his own profit (as every tenant who
fails in his farm, from want of industry or from drink or
other fault of his own, always represents himself as a martyr of
landlords' oppression); but, on the whole, personal and very inferior secondary motives are more powerful than religious. Even
in elections for Parliament, in every succeeding election money
is becoming more influential. In boroughs, neither side can get
many of their men to vote without it. Virtuous Protestants
will not stir for their own side till they have been paid, and the
Priests cannot move those of whose allegiance there is no doubt
till they have got the money. The answer, ' Why should we not
get it as well as another ? ' is conclusive, and a candidate who
will pay has to be found. In county elections the enormous
sums that have to be paid, sooner or later, to some one make
the chance of a man who cannot afford a great outlay a very
poor one, except in special circumstances. Small personal
profits are all powerful in Ireland. In the county of Cork, from
its great size, some expenses of voters going to the poll are
allowed to be paid. At a late election fifty or sixty well-to-do
farmers offered their second votes on the day of polling to a
friend of mine who was known to them, for whichever candidate he liked, if he would get them their expenses—some 3s. or
4s. per head !

It is the same between landlord and tenant. As one who has
never taken any active part in politics in Ireland, perhaps my
statement may be thought worth something, that not one in ten
of those graphic stories of electors coerced to vote against their
religion has any truth in it. Wherever a landlord is trusted,
and is on ordinary terms of goodwill with his tenants, a large
majority are quite willing, without the smallest coercion, to vote
as he wishes, from gratitude, in the old definition of that word—
the expectation of favours to come. I do not mean exceptional
favours, but such as increased farms for themselves or their
children when openings occur, and other small and every-day
benefits. They make the most of the priest's pressure on them
to enhance the service to the landlord, and they talk loudly of
the landlord's pressure to justify themselves to the priest, and
all the time what they most care for is, some advantage direct
or indirect to themselves or their friends.

Neither the Anglican clergyman nor the Roman Catholic
priest meets with anything but civil treatment from those of the
religion of his rival. The Protestant may talk in private of the
misdoings of the Roman Catholic priest, but he treats him in
public with all the respect that could be wished; and, practically, any Roman Catholic priest of moderate views is one of

the most influential men in his district among Protestants as much as among his own people. On the other hand, when an Anglican clergyman is true and upright and conciliatory, he is liked and valued by the Roman Catholics about him much more than he would be by any sect of Protestant Dissenters. There is none of that religious bitterness towards him that politicians in England suppose to be appropriate. The badge of conquest grievance, as a reason against the Irish Church, is in truth an importation from England. The explanation simply is that the Needy Knife-grinder was not a more thorough despiser of abstract wrongs than are the lower orders of Irish Roman Catholics. No greater mistake was ever made than Mr. Bright's statement, that Roman Catholics bear especial ill-will towards clergymen and members of the Established Church, as compared with Protestant Dissenters. The very reverse is the fact. Ill-will is much more felt and more easily excited towards Methodists and Presbyterians than towards Church people. I do not mean this digression to apply to the general question, whether the Establishment is or is not just towards Roman Catholics? I refer only to the narrower point, What is the importance of Fenianism and the extent of disaffection in Ireland, which I am firmly convinced have been made to bear a weight and importance that by no means belongs to them.

This brings me to the main question: Is it the object to place the Irish Church at a great disadvantage for the future, by reducing it to a chaos, and leaving it to its chance of reconstructing itself as well as it can? or is it the object only to get rid of Protestant ascendancy, and the exclusive privileges and anomalies of the Irish Church, and yet to recognise all fair and honest rights, and give it every chance of doing well for the future? Much depends upon which alternative is that really aimed at.

One great objection against the Irish Church is that it is the Church of the wealthiest part of the people. Dr. A. or Mr. B. has travelled in Ireland and gone to churches where he saw no poor; and he generalises accordingly. But, in truth, his induction is from insufficient facts. In much the larger number of country parishes the great majority are poor, and had Dr. A. gone to any number of parish churches he could not have helped seeing them. In many churches in England—especially those a traveller would be likely to visit—very few or no poor might be seen. I believe the proportion is little larger in Ireland, where the same thing occurs.

But, in truth, the wealth of the wealthy class in Ireland is very different from that of the same class in England. Setting

aside a few resident owners of great estates, the bulk of the
upper classes are far less wealthy than in England. There are
twenty men (if I said twice twenty, I should perhaps not ex-
aggerate), in districts of like extent, with incomes of 1,000*l.*
a year and over in England for one such in Ireland. 200*l.* to
500*l.* per annum is about the income of most of the gentry.
They are the very reverse of a rich body. Professional incomes,
except in great towns, are on the same scale. A shopkeeper
clearing 100*l.* to live on is considered well to do. Except in
the neighbourhood of a few large towns, it is a thoroughly poor
country. Wherever there is any number of Protestants, the
mass are tradesmen, farmers, and labourers, no better off than
the Roman Catholics around them of like occupations. It is
the numbers and system of the Roman Catholic Church, the
indispensable requirement of outward rites and church offices,
and of payment for them, that make the incomes of some of
their clergy so large. What voluntaryism can yield is shown by
the amount the Wesleyans are able to raise for their ministers.
Their hold is wholly among the shopkeepers. They have
hardly any poor. Lately, a wealthy member offered a large
sum, provided the salaries of their ministers in the South of
Ireland were raised, the unmarried to 40*l.* per annum, and the
married to 100*l.* It was some time before even such an offer
could be accepted, and this was thought a great advance! The
Presbyterians have the same difficulty in providing for their
clergy. Except in Ulster and the large towns, their ministers,
even with the help of the *Regium Donum*, are very poorly
paid, and have great trouble to sustain themselves. Whatever
the Church may suffer from disendowment, the loss of the
Regium Donum will be a much worse blow to the Presbyterians
in Three of the provinces.

In Ireland, all charities involving much cost, as hospitals,
even in the largest cities, which in England depend wholly on
voluntary support, invariably require and receive help from
rates or from Parliament. They could not exist without it,
simply because there is not a large enough wealthy class to give
to them.

Money is much more scarce in Ireland than in England, and
for that reason is much more thought of, and more grudgingly
expended. There is very little of that free spending, as if cost
was no object. Mere cost is carefully weighed, and inferior
and shabby makeshifts are constantly put up with, rather than
incur outlay, and that by people in almost every rank. This
will tell heavily on contributions for the clergy.

It is overlooked that the state in which a religious body is
placed by the withdrawal of its endowments is very different

from that in which it would have been if it had never had such endowments at all. To say nothing of the gifts of good men that would have accumulated in past years had no endowments existed, the duty of giving to the support of the ministers of any religion has to be learnt, and when just the opposite habits have been engrained for centuries, it will be long before these are unlearnt and the duty be recognised. It is just the case of emigrants in the colonies. They have not been used at home to pay their clergy, and the complaints are loud and constant of the impossibility of getting them to do so. The lower classes of Protestants in Ireland have been used to get help in all ways from the clergy, and it will take generations before they will have learnt to pay, instead of to receive. The habits of 300 years cannot quickly be changed.

A man reduced from wealth to poverty is in a very different state from one who has never been otherwise than poor, and has numberless difficulties of which the other knows nothing. It is certain non-resident owners of property will give little; it is only from residents that much help can be looked for. These, however, will have to pay their tithes to the Government as before. Such of them as care little for religion will think that enough, while with all but a few, the pressure of the old payment will unavoidably stint the measure of the performance of the new and additional duty.

It is, therefore, quite plain that if the tithe rent charge continues to be payable to the Government or any one else, and the Church is at the same time left dependent on the voluntary contributions of the rent charge payers, it will be thereby subjected to a great additional disadvantage, compared with its position if the rent charge was simply abolished or its payment made no longer compulsory by law, like Church rates in England. What would have been thought of a settlement of the Church rate question that forced English Churchmen still to pay Church rates to the Government as before, and left them besides to pay for the upholding of their own churches? The legal position of Church rates in England with reference to landowners was substantially the same as that of tithe rent charge in Ireland, and the amount, 500,000l. a year, not long since levied for Church rates, is more than the revenue of the Irish Church from tithes. Six-sevenths of the rent charge are paid by members of the Church, and it will be impossible to avoid the feeling in their minds that in paying it to the Government, or to whatever new object Parliament appoints, they are in some sort discharging their whole duty in this respect. The money may be misappropriated, but the responsibility for that will be felt to rest with Parliament and not with the payers, as, in fact, it does. Let the position of tithe payers be fairly considered who have just paid their 50*l.* or 100*l.* tithe to the Government. Is it likely with the various demands on their incomes, whether they be large or small, that most men will be in a promising frame of mind for again putting their hands in their pockets for another 50*l.* or 100*l.* for their clergymen?

It is clear that for very many years—probably for generations —the Church will labour under the greatest disadvantages in these respects. Such a change is not equality in a fair race. Both may start level from one goal, but one is handicapped in weight with a vengeance.

Therefore, if the Church is to depend on pure voluntaryism, in common justice and fair play the old rent charge must be got rid of somehow. It may be sold to the rent charge payers, and no doubt, though a man may have paid the value for it, in some years the remembrance of the payment will have passed away, and there will not be this abiding wet blanket on his contributions to his clergyman. In Lord Morpeth's and every other scheme for Irish Church reform between 1834–1839, doing away with the rent charge by sale to the payers was an essential part. I believe there is no case, among all the confiscations of Church property in Europe, in which the tithes have been continued as a payment from the land.

This real difficulty is sure to turn up whenever the question comes to details. It is one that the strongest voluntaries must feel the force of, and which already leads many people to say, in spite of the little love there is for Irish landowners, that the only fair settlement, if there is to be secularisation and a voluntary system, is the same as that of Church rates in England, viz., that the rent charge should simply cease. There is not, and has not however been, any demand for such a settlement from the landowners. The difficulty will be avoided if a fair provision for the Irish Church is somehow still left, as seems to be thought by many is Mr. Gladstone's real view.

To make a clean sweep of the property of the Irish Church, except some glebes and churches, and then to turn it adrift to start *de novo*, is a more flagrant injustice than anything that can be alleged against its present privileges. It may suit the ends of party politics, but the moral sense of all men used to the principles of right and law, as understood among us hitherto revolts from it. Whatever may have been the origin of existing rights of property, even though direct injustice, yet it has always been recognised that enjoyment for a long lapse of time does confer a title that cannot with justice be set aside. Innocent people become interested, and the original question has got involved with other rights, in numberless ways, that make extrication impossible, except at the cost of a still greater injustice. Opportunities have been lost that can never be recovered, and to take away the property that has been even unjustly got does not place things *in statu quo*. Every Statute of limitation in fact rests on this principle. Such limitation is not only expedient, but it is just, or at least more just than its opposite would be.

No one can fail to see how this applies to the Irish Church if he will consider what Sir B. Guinness's over 150,000*l*. spent on St. Patrick's implies, as well as the large donations of private persons to the Bishop of Cork, and Lady Esmonde's proposed endowments and donations. It is certain that had the Irish Church hitherto been in poverty, it would have received very large endowments by donations and bequests from zealous members, and to strip it now of all its hitherto enjoyed property, is to put it in a worse position than it otherwise would have been in.

No inconsiderable part of the property of the Irish Church has, in reality, been acquired for it by its own members. Take the case of the glebes, for instance, which it seems to be considered a great merit not to take away. The glebe houses have nearly all been built in the present and last generation, and actually paid for, partly by the subscriptions of churchmen, but chiefly out of the pockets of the incumbents, with money that they would otherwise have spent on their private uses. It is the improvements the same men have made in the glebe lands that give them much more than half their present value. These glebe lands and houses therefore are in every sense the property of the Church.

Irish Church history is full of accounts of the recovery by its members, often at much personal cost and trouble, of Church property that would otherwise have been lost by lapsing into lay hands. Some reasonable consideration is surely due to such exertions. It would be a poor return to say, ' Though you saved all this property, none of it shall be left to your Church.'

It is strange too that it does not seem to be observed that the laity have rights in the property of the Irish Church. Its revenue does not belong in an unqualified sense to its ministers, high or low ; yet every pecuniary interest of theirs is to be respected, down to the parish clerks, but nothing is said of the rights of the laity.

I am old enough to remember when, if the Church was spoken of, everyone understood that the clergy were meant. Then came better knowledge, and it was recognised that the Church meant the whole body of clergy and laity combined, and that the clergy were only the ministers (in the true sense of that word) of the laity, and existed for their sake.

. From the tone that has been taken in discussing this question it might be thought that the old view was not exploded, and that the property of the Church really belonged in some proper sense to the clergy, the laity having nothing to do with it and no rights in it. The sparing of the present life interests of the clergy has been spoken of as if it was a concession to the Irish Church, as if it was leaving the largest part of its property in its own hands.

But this is a complete delusion. The securing of these life interests to the present clergy will be no advantage to the laity. If the property is, sooner or later, to be swept away, it would be more to their advantage that it should be done at once. It is quite a mistake that the gradual change by letting the present incumbents go on as they are till their parishes become vacant by death will be favourable to the Church. It will be only letting it die by inches. Such a course will hinder all enthusiasm. It will never be clear when the right time for an effort has come; in truth, the bitterest malice could contrive no plan more hurtful to the Church.

The necessary resource of the Church, whether its revenues are wholly taken away or only lessened, is in the grouping of the parishes—say by making a parish to consist of an area containing, on an average, 400 or 500 Protestants. But if the present incumbents go on as now, this grouping can only be effected when the last incumbent of the parishes to form the group dies. There will be no power to make the other incumbents do the duties of the parishes first vacant, which will be often laborious, such as Services and visiting the sick in distant places, &c. In the meantime all will be confusion and loss. Further, bishoprics must be grouped too, and should a bishop die soon (suppose the Bishop of Cork, the area of whose see is one-eighth of all Ireland), how are the duties of his diocese to be performed? Who is to superintend the needful arrangement of grouping parishes, when a chance occurs at the critical time? How is an adjoining bishop, or a new bishop (is he to be elected, and by whom? to suppose possibilities) to get jurisdiction over the old incumbents, or to use it, during the 30 years or more they will be dying out? This grouping must therefore be done at once.

No doubt it is possible to make these life interests a means of helping to provide for the Church of the future. But this can only be done by fit arrangements for that end, and without such arrangements no advantage will accrue to the laity by sparing these life interests.

Tithe rent charge is commonly spoken of as an annuity, subject to which landowners or their ancestors bought their estates, and in respect to which annuities they have consequently no rights. But this is by no means a true statement of the case, especially where the landowners are resident. In such case it is clearly an annuity for which the payer receives a consideration in return, by the performance of the services of religion for himself, his family, and dependents. This consideration very materially affects his residential position. It has a clear pecuniary value, the amount of which there is no difficulty in fixing. It is just what would have to be paid to procure these religious services as well and conveniently.

Men's minds are familiar with the idea of advowsons being bought and sold, and so being a species of property, and therefore no question is made that the owners of advowsons are to be compensated. But, surely, to deprive a man of the right of appointing a clergyman to a parish is to deprive him of a much less real and personal interest, and that right is in its nature much less of an 'individual right of property,' both in the words and sense of the Resolutions, than to deprive him altogether of the services of a parish clergyman—the very consideration in his favour, subject to which he has always paid his tithes—the legal consideration of the annuity charged on the land he or his ancestor bought ?

If the case was one between man and man, of money to be paid by one and services rendered by the other, there could not be a moment's doubt of the rights and the law. If an estate was bought in England charged with an annuity in favour of a schoolmaster or dissenting minister for his services in any place, whether the origin of the arrangement was prescription or an express deed, there is no sort of doubt the Court of Chancery would enforce the condition; and if the services were withheld, the owner of the estate would not be bound to pay the annuity. It is quite clear he did not buy subject to a simple annuity, but to an annuity on condition of services to be performed. Those services, whether secular or religious, are a benefit to him, and he has a clear equitable right to them, which on every recognised principle of property he cannot be deprived of without compensation.

If, indeed, Parliament thought fit to make over the annuity to the Roman Catholic parish priest, there might be the answer, that the religious services were there in another form for the payer of the annuity, if he liked to avail himself of them. But if Parliament appropriates the money to the secular purposes of the State it represents—i.e., to itself—the claim for compensation becomes irresistible. If the question could be argued before any Court of Equity without the technical difficulties and the prejudices that exist, the result would not be doubtful.

. The words of the Resolutions of last Session are, 'That it is necessary the Established Church of Ireland should cease to exist as an Establishment, due regard being paid to all personal interests and to all individual rights of property;' and whenever the details of the measure come to be considered, I think it will be impossible to contend that the rights of resident tithe payers who have bought land under such conditions do not fairly come within the words, 'personal interests.'

It is no answer to say that if the money is applied to education the tithe payer will profit by that. When property is taken for a railway, the man from whom it is taken profits by the line as much, and often more, than his neighbour whose land is untouched. But he is paid for his land nevertheless, because he is deprived of something, whilst his neighbour is not deprived of anything. The case of the resident tithe payer who is deprived of the services of religion is just analogous.

Many resident laymen have, however, a further claim than this. Many have spent large sums on Churches and for Church purposes, in the full confidence that, though the present *status* of the Church might not remain, yet the substance would be so far preserved as would still endure for the purposes for which their money was given. It was felt that the sweeping away of endowments from parishes where congregations are numbered by scores and hundreds (there are many such parishes in Ireland) involves the whole question of religious endowments in England and Scotland, and could not be carried out in Ireland, except on principles that would equally strip those Churches—viz., on the principle of the superiority of voluntaryism.

The case of one by no means wealthy layman is within my knowledge, who in the past twelve years has laid out in this confidence nearly 3,000*l*.: 2,100*l*. in building a new church, 500*l*. towards a new cathedral, and 300*l*. towards a glebe house in another parish, besides being security for a further 400*l*. borrowed to build that house. The motive was by no means sectarian, but to help in raising the state of religion, by enabling the services of God to be performed with decent fitness, instead of in buildings where every association was common and mean. The glebe house was to secure a resident clergyman as a means of goodwill and charity to Protestants and Roman Catholics alike, in a parish where there was no house in which even a curate could dwell. And the goodwill hoped for has resulted now for several years. It was not expected the Irish Church would remain as it was, but the continuance of moderate endowment, in some way, where a good congregation existed, was never doubted, and such endowment was the felt and implied consideration upon which the money was given. The advowson of the parish where the church is built is private property. It may be worth about half the money spent upon the church. It was bought for mere lucre's sake. Yet its owner is to be compensated, and discharged from the condition in favour of the builder of the church upon which he has hitherto held his property, of nominating a minister who shall perform the duties of the parish.

But it will be said such cases are rare. I can only speak of the diocese I know. The bishop of it has within a few years had the sums of 17,000*l*. and 10,000*l*. placed at his disposal by two laymen for Church purposes. Half of these sums has been spent in the past six years on churches and glebes within the diocese, and the remainder elsewhere. In addition, 23,500*l*. more has been subscribed in the diocese for the same objects by private persons, mostly laymen; making 37,000*l*. in all in six years spent on one diocese alone.

It may be said these sums were spent on churches and glebes of which it is not proposed to deprive the Church. But the true consideration, in a legal sense, on which these sums were given was the existing endowment for a clergyman to perform the duty of the parish, to which the church and glebe are mere accessories and aids. If this consideration is now otherwise appropriated, the right of compensation is in justice as complete as can be. What will be the use of church and glebe without a clergyman?

It is often said the Irish Church has vastly improved in the past quarter of a century. It is forgotten that that improvement has shown itself in substantial good works, and that if it is to be deprived of that which alone makes those works of any benefit, it has at least a right out of its former revenues to the actual outlay as a help towards a future provision.

I am convinced there will be found an overwhelming preponderance of the opinions of all men used to weigh questions of Law and Equity in favour of the justice of this claim. It already has in its favour the opinions of two such lawyers of opposite politics as Lord Cairns and Sir R. Palmer. In questions of this kind, even doubtful rights have to be conceded; much more cannot rights be refused that rest on sound and acknowledged principles and everyday practice.

When negro slavery was abolished, compensation was given for the claims of slave owners to the amount of twenty millions, paid out of the national purse. These claims were derived from cruelty and immorality, and were contrary to every principle of moral right. Compared with them the claims of Protestant laymen to pay the tithes of the land they own to their own Church must be innocent and meritorious in the eyes even of the strongest opponents of the Irish Church. How, then, can the compensation that was given in the one case be withheld in the other? No one can doubt that a large pecuniary burden will be put on the resident tithe payer, who is a member of the Church, and to this extent his claim is just. He may not, indeed, claim to be paid compensation in money, but he claims that in the arrangements on the subject his rights shall be fairly taken into account.

There is also another most important practical question. Admitting that the Church is to be deprived of exclusive privileges of every kind that affect any outside her communion, what good reason is there for depriving her of those legal rights that her members now have as between themselves? This is quite a different question from that of Establishment, though often confounded with it. All religious bodies in the kingdom, in fact, have some such legal rights.

When the rights of any dissenting body come before the Courts, whether those rights depend on the intention of a testator, or upon the law of contract, express or implied, those rights are thereby recognised by law. When the Court of Chancery, in the case of Lady Hewley's charity, investigated the differing doctrines of different sections of such a dissenting body, it recognised rights by law to exist in such body. So when the courts at Natal decided whether Dr. Colenso or the incumbent of a church was entitled to its use, they were clearly recognising existing legal rights of the members of the same church between themselves. Yet no one ever thought that the Church of Natal, or these dissenting bodies, thereby became Established Churches.

Further, the law of trusts in our courts is the very charter upon which every sort of religious body holds the most part of its endowments. The law of France does not permit such trusts even for the French Church, and the strong wish of earnest and intelligent French Roman Catholics (no one has spoken so strongly on the subject as M. de Montalembert) is that their Church might have the benefit of such a law. Here again such trusts are equitable rights recognised as existing in religious bodies by the law of the land, but having nothing to do with establishment.

Again the Queen appoints bishops to our colonial Churches and in India, and many chaplains in India are even paid by the Government, but this does not make the colonial or Indian Churches Established Churches.

If an Act of Parliament was to settle the rights of dissenting bodies that are now settled by the courts on the principles of Common Law or of equity, it would not thereby make them

Established Churches. After the decision of the Court of Chancery in Lady Hewley's case, such an Act was actually passed, without any such effect.

Is it not the truth that there has been no precise definition hitherto attached to the words Established Church? The expression, the Church by Law Established, is a description, not a definition, and has given rise in the minds of many to the impression (for it is no more) that any rights given by law to a Church make it thereby an Established Church. When this expression came into use, connection of a Church with the State, *i.e.*, Establishment, meant a very real support and the gift of very exclusive privileges in endowments and rank, &c. Any other body not the Established Church was in a sort of outlawry.

It is the recognition of these exclusive privileges, as against other bodies outside her communion, whether through the action of Church courts or otherwise, that constitutes the true idea of an Establishment, not the recognition by the Courts or by Act of Parliament of more or less legal rights in the members of a Church as between themselves. To take away the legal rights of the Irish Church as between its own members is simply to reduce it to a state of anarchy. This must have been Mr. Bright's idea when he talked of 1,000 or 500 members of the Irish Church holding a convention in Dublin to settle all its affairs *de novo*. It would be quite as easy to settle a new Social compact. The ideas needful for such a work are wholly wanting in Ireland, both among clergy and laity. Neither the one nor the other have the knowledge, or habits, or temper for it.

But even if it was otherwise, to reduce a Church that has hitherto had settled laws to a state of anarchy, and then leave it to reconstitute itself as it can on purely voluntary principles, is an ordeal such as no Church could go through without grievous injury. Such an upset and reconstruction is quite different from the gradual growth of a Church or religious body from small beginnings, under whatever disadvantages. It is to put a positive obstacle in the way of a most serious kind. Consider, too, the preliminary questions that have to be settled. Who are to sit in such a convention? What clergy? What laity? What shadow of power would they have to regulate any questions, unless power was given them by Act of Parliament, which would, in substance, thereby settle the whole business? Conceive a convention in Ireland of all who liked to attend, with the Orange element uppermost, or every man with a crotchet, either on doctrine, or discipline, or ceremonies, urging it to the uttermost, as he would have a right to do. What authority, unless conferred by an Act of Parliament, would there be to hold even an acre of glebe land, much less to do any other legal act?

The colonial Churches afford no precedent. Their circumstances were quite different. At first the colonial clergy were paid mainly by Societies at home, and were under the direction of those societies. When bishops were appointed, such Churches were still in their infancy. The bishop was the channel through which the Societies at home chiefly acted; he held the purse-strings, and had thus great influence over the clergy. The Church in the colony in this way grew up gradually from a small beginning.

The law of contract and the law of trusts are held in substance now to regulate the rights of the bishops and clergy and laity of such Churches among themselves in all that relates to jurisdiction and control, as well as to endowments. It is the same with dissenting bodies; the laws of contract and trusts really govern them too.

But the Irish Church has to get from the one state to the other—from being governed by the laws that now govern it, to another state under the laws of contract and trusts. For thirty to fifty years there will be some bishops and clergy under the old laws, and free from all contracts or trusts, and others working under quite a different system, and unless by Act of Parliament power is given to adjust those two systems, they cannot help clashing. When a bishop dies, the bishop appointed in his place, suppose by voluntary election, will have no authority over the old incumbents. If the bishop should die soon after the change has taken place, there may be no voluntary clergy, or only two or three in the diocese, for him to preside over. The old incumbents, except by Act of Parliament, cannot be brought under the new law of contract, and if the Act of Parliament has to define the new contract, it will have a very tough job—nothing less than to make a new code of ecclesiastical law.

Nor, as far as I can see, is there any way out of this difficulty, unless it is admitted that the rights of the members of the Church, *as between themselves*, shall continue. If that is admitted, then the Act of Parliament may make the old law of the Church to that extent binding upon its members, as if it had been a contract between themselves, and until altered, by whatever authority, as of a synod, shall hereafter have control over the affairs of the Church. I believe there is no objection in principle to such an Act, and to refuse it would be to subject the Church, as I have said, to an ordeal of difficulties. Without a start of this kind, the Church will not have fair play. Special provisions can alone adjust the relations of the old system with a new system. It will else be in the power of individual perversity, or temper, or fancy, wherever such exist, to bring everything to a dead lock.

The sum of the whole is, that an equitable compromise is the only practicable course. As long as men keep to generals, and look only at one side of the case, nothing is so easy as doing away with the Irish Church. Directly they condescend to particulars, and are forced to look at what is just to both sides, every step carries them into greater difficulties, which can only be settled fairly by compromise.

Such a compromise is for the interest of all parties. The proposed plan of equally stripping the Church of its revenues, the Roman Catholics of the Maynooth grant and the Presbyterians of the *Regium Donum*, can rightly be described as resting on no other principle than that of mutual hatred.

Its only claims on each denomination are that it will injure its neighbour. It may be welome to the bitter Roman Catholic, because it will hurt the Church. It may be welcome to the bitter Protestant, because he knows the loss of the Maynooth grant will be keenly felt by the Roman Catholic—and already it is said the ill-omened words are heard in the North: 'At any rate, in future we need keep no terms with Papists'—whilst the ultra-Presbyterian may rejoice in the loss to both the others.

While extreme and violent men are more or less content, the reasonable and moderate men of all parties are correspondingly dissatisfied. It ought to be distinctly understood that it is upon these moderate men, of all parties, that the peace and progress of the country depend. It is not too much to say that the very first object of all their doings is to keep down and get rid of all mutual hatred, and to encourage goodwill in its place, as the condition of any moral and social good in the country. In truth, the encouragement of goodwill between men of different parties and religions ought to be the first end considered in every measure for Ireland. So far as changes affecting the interests or feelings of any class are necessary, no sacrifice in the mode of carrying them out is too great, if it attains this end. There is this great help, that compromise is much more congenial to the Irish mind than to the English. That stiff backbone and grasp of his rights so common in the English is very much wanting in the Irish, and the loudest and fiercest declarations are always to be understood with the implied reservation that they are not 'the last words,' and are often only meant to help towards getting better terms in the foreseen settlement.

That which is most wanting in Ireland is that Protestants and

Roman Catholics should in matters of religion look on each other as fellow Christians. Of course intelligent men do not deny this in words when the question is put to them, but the practice on both sides is to act as if it was otherwise. It would not so much matter if they would even look on each other as erring Christians, provided only they really felt each other to be Christians at all. The result is very discreditable to both religions. Any schemer who professes himself a convert and reviles his former religion is treated as a good Protestant. On the other hand, the efforts to get the priest to a dying Protestant, in whatever state of weakness and half-consciousness, if so be he may profess himself a Roman Catholic, are enough to justify the charge that Roman Catholics believe salvation and damnation are in the priest's hands. It is very desirable therefore that nothing should be done that will give a triumph to one side or the other.

Moreover, this plan of tearing up everything by the roots on both sides, whether it has existed for centuries or has been the deliberate action of Parliament approved by some of the greatest men the country ever had, and starting instead a brannew arrangement on wholly different principles, is necessarily destructive of confidence. Next to peace and goodwill, confidence is that which is most wanted in Ireland. Even in England, though it may suit a section of the Radical mind to talk of such a course, it is contrary to all the traditions and feelings of the people. The steady improvement and reform of existing institutions is the end sought by sober men of ever so advanced opinions, not the destruction of such institutions and invention of new ones in their stead. In the social state of Ireland this loss of confidence will be most hurtful; it will do unmixed mischief. If it is needful for the sake of three-fourths of the Irish people to displace the Irish Church from its position, it is not for the good of the kingdom to do so in such a way as will needlessly aggravate and outrage one-fourth of its most intelligent and loyal subjects. Religious strife unhappily is not hard to stir up, and may be stirred up from either side; witness the Belfast riots three years ago.

A compromise is for the interest of Roman Catholics. Whatever hurt they may succeed in doing to the Irish Church, the Roman Catholics may be sure they will not get rid of it. It will not be for their advantage to have its clergy forced on the support of proselytising Societies in England, with Exeter Hall as headquarters. It is said, on good Roman Catholic authority, that no less than 80,000*l.* a year is now spent, one way or another, for this purpose by English Societies. One such Society undoubtedly spends over 30,000*l.* per annum in proselytising in Ireland. It has not hitherto been very successful (with one notable exception), because the common sense of Irish Protestants living among Roman Catholics is too strong, except in times of excitement, and compels them to make peace their first object.

If the mind of the great religious party in England that now supports the Society alluded to should be thoroughly roused, and much larger funds be subscribed (the same party already raises four or five times 30,000*l.* a year with no great effort for another of its Societies, and it is at least possible might largely increase its efforts to proselytise in Ireland), and if at the same time there was an ill-paid and poor clergy with wives and children dependent, the result may easily be imagined. What has been done in West Connaught is at least possible elsewhere, and the excessive fear and hatred of proselytism the Roman Catholic clergy show at all times is not without its significance.

Neither is it well that a direct pecuniary motive should be given to landlords to prefer Protestant tenants, or that there should be even a suspicion of such a motive. At present no one of sense or intelligence makes any difference. Will it be so when a constant struggle has to be carried on to support a clergyman, and the subscription of every well-to-do farmer will lighten the burden on the landowner of a few hundreds per annum? Putting aside every unworthy motive, I believe there is a source here of abiding bitterness.

It is not many years ago since the Maynooth grant was deliberately increased by Sir Robert Peel, because it was for the good of all alike that the future Roman Catholic clergy should not undergo during their training the coarse hard life that the poverty of the College had previously compelled, but should have the benefit of the civilising effects of more refined habits.

I do not think that any one who knows practically the exceedingly rough material out of which the Roman Catholic clergy are formed can doubt that this step was dictated by the soundest judgment.

The Maynooth students are the sons of farmers and others whose previous lives have been passed in the low habits of humble Irish boys of their class, without one idea fitting them for the position of clergymen of any denomination. Every thought that is to raise them above their fellows, of whom they are to be the guides, must be got at the College. Can there be any doubt that it is desirable the habits of that College should be of a civilising and refining tendency? Yet all this is now overlooked.

. As a mere matter of State wisdom, is it wise to allow religious partisans to avail themselves of coarseness and poverty, and work them up into furious bigotry? Let the example, too, and the unsettling effect of depriving the Roman Catholics of what was so solemnly and with so much consideration given them, for the very purpose of securing the grant from future dispute, by the greatest Conservative statesman of these times, and with the applause of the whole Liberal party and of a great majority of Parliament, be considered. There has surely been no previous instance of the reversal of such deliberately conferred rights. No matter what the excuse, ought such a course to be taken by the British Parliament?

Doubtless the Roman Catholics will not allow Maynooth to fall, but the difficulty of raising money, even with their numbers and organisation, for an additional and distant object is great; and the same poverty as before Sir R. Peel's increased payment will unavoidably be its lot. It is little known how much personal influence and exertion have to do with the money the Roman Catholic clergy now raise. It is the fact that every extra demand, even that of late years for the Pope, is most heavily felt and disliked by the Roman Catholic farmers and others on whom the burden falls. Let it be observed, too, that this is proposed to be done when, as the Maynooth grant and *Regium Donum* are not very different in amount, equality, to that extent at least, could be obtained by leaving an equivalent share of its revenues to the Church; so that it would be a purely wanton mischief, resting on no principle except that of mere voluntaryism.

I feel bound to add, that there is a further concession that I think Roman Catholics may fairly claim in the event of a compromise. Mr. Gregory, member for Galway, in his speech on the state of Ireland, in March 1868, urges that a glebe house and some acres of land ought to be provided for every Roman Catholic clergyman. This proposal was first made by O'Connell, and it was strongly pressed by Mr. Bright, so long ago as 1852. It deserves far more notice than it received amidst the din of party warfare. The cost will be so small, and the actual value in money will be so trifling, that it can hardly be called an endowment. It will scarcely be more than, after the tithe-war of 1832–3, was contemptuously tossed to the Irish clergy for the relief of their distress, because they could not collect their tithes. Of course the value of a house and a few acres of land is something, yet it is not a great addition to such incomes as many of the Roman Catholic clergy now possess. The motive for such a gift in a great settlement of this kind is as a proof of goodwill and conciliatory feelings. No one can object more than I do to truckling to the Roman Catholic clergy, or any approach to it. I think there is often too much of such truckling on the part of Government, and of many men who at other times express very strong Protestant opinions. I believe the Roman Catholic clergy should be opposed in a manly, straightforward way, more strongly than they are generally now opposed, when they are in the wrong, as they often are. I am quite alive to the unjustifiable pretensions and overbearing conduct of some of the Roman Catholic clergy (especially in the high places in their Church); and whatever may be said against the undue influence of landlords over tenants, the undue influence used by the Roman Catholic clergy for election purposes is quite beyond that used by anyone else in the Three kingdoms, and would raise a shriek of reprobation from the Liberal party if it was used against them. But I believe none the less that the greater number of the Roman Catholic clergy are the friends of law and order. I think their influence, on the whole, is used in favour of right; and though occasionally individuals make themselves conspicuous in a bad sense, yet the majority are worthy and charitable men, doing their duty in their station in proportion to their lights, and that the country owes much to them. In the late Fenian excitement, so far as my observation extended, I can bear witness that the conduct of the Roman Catholic clergy was deserving of every praise. No doubt the American Fenians were as hostile to the influence of the Roman Catholic clergy as to that of the British Government; but this is one of those happy coincidences which it is for a wise Government to take advantage of, especially as it is certain the Roman Catholic clergy feel that they deserve well of the Government in this instance.

A house and a few acres of land—a house of their own for their lives—is the one thing within reach that would add to the contentment and enjoyment of these men. It could in no way interfere with their influence, or add to it. It is not valuble enough to be thought of as a bribe. It is a personal gratification, in the good sense of the word, to men whose lives have not too much of enjoyments of any sort. It could be perverted to no ill end. Such an opportunity may never occur again. It should by no means be lost. now. Done under present circumstances, it will be no precedent. If the glebes are to be left to the Irish Church, it will be mere equality. Above all, it will tend strongly to promote peace and quiet in the land. How much it will be prized may be judged from an advertisement that, whilst I write, has appeared in one of the Cork newspapers:

 33

'LORD LISLE AND HIS TENANTRY.

'*To the Editor of the* CONSTITUTION.

' Dear Sir,—Your readers who.have seen your report of the public rejoicings in honour of Lord Lisle, and the cordial welcome given him on the occasion of his auspicious arrival among his tenantry in this and the adjoining parishes, will not be unprepared to hear acts of liberality and kindness at his hands.

'His lordship has shown the sincerity of his liberal professions in many instances, one of which, intimately concerning myself and my parishioners, I feel called upon in gratitude to bring under the notice of the public through the columns of your journal. Some days since he did my curate, the Rev. S. O'Donnell, who has the good fortune of being one of his lordship's tenants, the honour of a visit. He inquired how much land he held, how much rent he paid; and being informed that his lot contained seven acres Irish, at a rent of 7l. 10s. a year, he, with a munificence worthy of his high title, made him and his successors a present of his little farm. He also inquired was the parish priest's house on his property, and when answered in the negative, he appeared to regret that he had not an opportunity of complimenting him in a similar handsome manner. Would that we had many such landlords in poor, unhappy Ireland. We would not then hear of such harrowing scenes as have lately sent a thrill of horror through the heart of the country. That Lord Lisle may enjoy his title and ancestral estates for many a long year is the fervent prayer of the priests and people of this district.—Yours truly,

'C. O'CONNELL, P.P.

' Meelin : September 1, 1868.'

A compromise is for the good of the Anglican Church. The present state of things is not satisfactory in any respect. In many cases the grouping of parishes will be a gain to the Church, and not a loss. Parishes with congregations of 3 or 5, or 10 or 20 souls, are a scandal, and do harm. Even where the parishioners number from 100 to 200, the Church will thrive better with a larger parish and more parishioners. 20 or 40 families do not give half work to a clergyman; at first, probably, he tries to make work, but soon finds everything can be done in one or two days a week, and the result is by no means good on his own character or on his people.

On the other hand, the strife of proselytism under a voluntary system relying for help on English Societies, and the evils

C

of a dependent clergy, are not favourable to the true character of the Church or to her usefulness. Whatever other fruit the Church of Ireland has hitherto produced, I have long been convinced by observation that it has influenced the Roman Catholics in Ireland for good, and does so still, amidst whatever drawbacks. The observation of the Archbishop of Dublin, in his late Charge, that the pressure of the Church has made our Lord's Atonement a much more prominent article of faith among Irish Roman Catholics than among those of other parts of Europe, is in my opinion quite true. They have felt the pinch in the controversy, of having to defend the worship of the Virgin and Saints; and however romantic minds may satisfy themselves with reasons in favour of such practices, the common sense of large numbers in Ireland is against them, and not half the prominence is given to such doctrines as in other Roman Catholic countries. It is the same with reading the Bible. The common sense of the more intelligent Roman Catholics will not bear to be deprived of it, and numbers of them possess and read it, of course in their own version. Another instance is the tone of the better sort as to the manner in which Sunday should be kept. They constantly keep it and speak of it in a way that no reasonable Protestant can dissent from, and wholly different from that in which it is viewed in other Roman Catholic countries. I think the same influence obtains on other points of morality, and if religious bitterness could be lessened, would do so more and more. This is the true work and field of labour of the Irish Church in regard to Roman Catholics.

I do not put any faith in the assertions of the benefit of disestablishment ; nor, on the other hand, do I believe in the extraordinary virtues Mr. Gladstone is in the habit of ascribing to the Irish clergy. But I think that anything that compels the clergy to more work will be eminently useful to the Church.

This brings me to the question, In what way can a compromise be effected ?

It is quite plain no help from the general taxation of the country can be expected. It would not be endured, even if it was reasonable. But one source of money has been overlooked, which, with the help of some time and patience, is capable of yielding any amount that is wanted—I mean the surplus annual revenue of the Irish Church itself. Let it be supposed that the proposal of last session was carried out simply as a matter of finance. The life interests proposed to be left to the present incumbents will take thirty years for the bulk of them to run out—i.e., before the present state of things will have passed substantially away; and as they would begin to fall in at once, unless the reversions were sold, the accruing total from the revenues of these vacant benefices would, by the end of these thirty years, amount to a very large sum—to half the total net income multiplied by the thirty years. If the net income of the Irish Church is 600,000*l.* per annum, such surplus will in thirty years amount to nine millions without the interest, which could be used to supply present needs. If the net income is more than 600,000*l.*, this surplus will be so much more. In this way the surplus revenues of the Church in time will give any amount of money that may be desired for effecting any sort of compromise in favour of any religious body, and in any proportions.

When so long a period as thirty years is unavoidable to bring the present state of things substantially to an end (and probably twenty years more wholly to do so), surely some time more or less is of little moment, nor can it matter in a national point of view, whilst these years are running out, whether the accruing surplus is applied to the purposes of a compromise or to the secular objects that are to be its ultimate end. It is clear that out of this accruing surplus a provision may be made for the Church, to whatever extent is judged reasonable—to that of Mr. Gladstone's three-fifths, or any other. A few years more would provide for the Maynooth grant and *Regium Donum.* And at the end of the period the whole present ecclesiastical revenues of Ireland would be available for whatever objects were judged best.

Of course, if that form of compromise is preferred, it can be made in the way of a purchase of the life interests of the clergy and other rights that all agree are to be spared; and in the same way a purchase of the Maynooth grant and *Regium Donum* can be made. The purchase-money can be paid out of this accruing surplus, with some arrangement as to the interest in the meantime. A very moderate share of the liberality that has been so largely promised would get over any difficulties. The affair could be arranged much as was done in Canada, when the clergy reserves were taken from the Church there, and the life interests in them bought up by the Government, the purchase-money being paid over to the Church for its after-support.

Or it might be done by allowing a certain number of years of grace to the Church after each benefice becomes vacant, during which the tithes of the parish should accumulate for a future provision.

Surely some such plan as this is preferable to mere destruction. The object is to leave the Church reasonably provided for, and yet remove the whole bone of contention, the *corpus* of the endowments of the Irish Church. So long as endowments of any sort are permitted to any Church, there can be no objection on principle to such a compromise.

The arrangement about the Canada clergy reserves is not generally known. The Canadian Government acted with great liberality to the Church, in regard to the life interests of the clergy in the reserves. The Government offered to buy up those life interests, at such a rate of purchase, that when the purchase-money was re-invested in the colony at the ordinary rate of interest current there on landed security, it produced in perpetuity as large an income as the clergy gave up. The purchase-money was paid to the Bishop and Church Society in trust, and invested by them accordingly. Neither the Church nor the clergy lost anything.

It was no mere actuaries' valuation of the life interests, but a bonâ fide liberal treatment of the Church at large, securing her against voluntaryism and a poor clergy, whilst getting rid of the political difficulty of an establishment and endowment from the public estate. The diocese of Montreal alone has 23,000l. per annum endowment left for less than 100 clergy. And if the Irish Church is treated according to this precedent, or anything like it, it will have little to complain of in a money point of view.

No doubt there are many to whom it will seem a great object so to clench the question, that the Roman Catholic Church may never in future times have a chance of acquiring any of these revenues. I think such a feeling is very narrow and unworthy. At present, public opinion is against giving these revenues to the Roman Catholics. But the revenues are not yet available for any purpose. The life interests have yet to run out, and will take thirty years in doing so. To dispose of these future accruing revenues now, or to dissipate them, is for the present to forestall a future generation. When these revenues have accrued, if the public opinion of that time is the same as that at present, Roman Catholics will get none of the money. If more goodwill and more united feelings have by that time increased, as we are told the disestablishment of the Irish Church will increase them, this generation will by such a course be only making a difficulty for the next. If public opinion is then in favour of the justice or expediency of in some way endowing the Roman Catholic Church, the money for the purpose will have to be found elsewhere, and the endowment will be made all the same. It was no small wisdom that said, 'Sufficient unto the day is the evil thereof.' The Irish Church is quite big enough a job without deciding on the disposition of its revenues thirty years hence. Even if the revenues are to be applied to secular objects, they will be applied with ten times more effect when they have accumulated than if applied by driblets as they accrue; and in calmer times, and after more consideration, they will be disposed of for much better objects than now that they are the sport of party in a moment of excitement.

Some details will show that a compromise is more practicable than is believed by many. The present net revenue of the Irish parochial clergy amounts to no more than 366,262*l.* per annum. The ecclesiastical commissioners, the bishops, and the deans and chapters absorb the residue of the income, making up about 600,000*l.* in all. If, as some say, it is 700,000*l.* per annum, the case is so much the stronger.

But 366,262*l.* is so exactly between the three-fifths and two-thirds of 600,000*l.*, that Mr. Gladstone at first stated his proposal would leave to the Church, that it is hard to believe he was not aware of the fact when he committed himself to that proportion. If otherwise, it is a singular chance he should have arrived at a sum which, if made over in any form bonâ fidê to the Church and not to the clergy as individuals, will so simplify the difficulty. The Church would have to provide for the life interests of the bishops, of the deans and chapters, &c., and it would have to take on itself the charges now *borne by the ecclesiastical commissioners.

But the 366,262*l.* includes all the parishes that ought to be grouped from smallness of numbers, &c.; and by such grouping at once, by compromises with incumbents, and other expedients hereafter to be stated, enough could be raised to meet the incomes present and future of the bishops and others, whilst the present charges of the commissioners could be raised by subscription.

These figures have been taken from the Report of the Commission on the Irish Church. That they should show any such plan, even to approach to being practicable, is a clear proof that everything depends for the Church on the manner in which the change is made. All turns on the subject proposed, whether good or ill to the Church is really meant by Mr. Gladstone's words, whether the three-fifths is a reality or a fiction.

Over and over again Liberals great and small have declared that it is not at all a question of money. The utmost liberality has been repeatedly promised. It is certain the more intelligent Roman Catholics have no wish to see the Church stripped of its revenues beyond a certain point. An endowment of at least 200,000*l.* a year is the amount that has been stated to me by such men as the sum they wished to see left. If the Irish Church is not to be sacrificed to the present generation of its own clergy, if it is not the object to subject it to the evils and difficulties of voluntaryism in the future, it is plain how a reasonable compromise can be attained.

Another motive for a compromise, that has not been yet fairly considered, is that there are parts of the revenues of the Irish Church to which, on plain grounds of right and justice, it has the clearest title. I think it must have surprised every one to read the way in which Mr. Gladstone lately in Lancashire spoke of leaving to the Irish Church endowments made by private persons, and the glebes and churches built in no small part out of the personal income of churchmen. It was put forward as a great concession that these were to be left, although, in truth, it is no concession at all.

They rest on the same grounds of common right as the private gifts of Roman Catholics to their Church, which we are told have amounted to five millions of money in no great number of years past. The Church has an indisputable right to all such endowments from private persons. Such is Primate Boulter's fund and the many additions to livings that have been made from it. The income of the fund now exceeds 6,000*l.* a year. There are similar funds bequeathed by others, but of smaller amount.

Such donations also as that of Sir B. Guinness have the strongest claim to respect, as well as many others of smaller amount. It is not good for the cause of right and truth in the land that private liberality of this sort should be rendered nugatory by the action of Parliament. Without the endowments heretofore supporting Divine Service in the churches that have thus been built, these churches will be stripped of the consideration upon which their builders gave their money. There is a righteous claim that those endowments should be spared, or replaced by an equivalent from the surplus revenues of the Church. Where men have freely given to God's service, it is not wise to destroy the result of their labours for a small gain, still less in order to gratify the jealousy of those of a different religion.

There is also the question of the advowsons. Here, though the patron has the right of presenting to the living, surely the parishioners have their rights also. The patron may continue to present to the new parish of which the value of the advowson helps to provide the endowment, but the parish ought not to be deprived of that valûe.

Everybody too must feel that there is a wide difference between the Pre-Reformation and Post-Reformation endowments. Whatever claim Roman Catholics can urge to the tithes—whether they did or did not once belong to their Church, or whether they were first given to a Church of which we have as much right to be considered the lawful successors as they have, it is beyond all question that to endowments of the Church since the Reformation they have no such claim. The grants of Elizabeth and James to the Irish Church were large. They were deliberately and knowingly made for the benefit of the Church and the promotion of its Protestant principles, out of lands legally and justly, according to the views of those times, at the disposal of the Sovereign, and which would otherwise have been bestowed on individuals at the Sovereign's mere pleasure for private purposes.

The grant of 111,000 acres of glebes in Ulster was made by James I. at the same time as the grants of estates to the Companies of the City of London, which those companies now possess, and the title of which no one disputes.

The only possible ground for questioning the right of the Church to these grants, and the similar ones made by Elizabeth to Trinity College (which were also in reality grants for Church purposes, *i.e.*, for distinctively Church education, and intended so to be), is that they were grants by a Sovereign as such. But so were the grants of George III. at New York to the Church there, before the American revolution. These grants of King George now yield the Church at New York an endowment of over 100,000*l.* a year, a larger amount than the grants of Elizabeth and James together. Yet they have always been respected by a Republican government, in spite of attacks.

That they were grants from the Crown is therefore no sufficient reason for depriving the Church of them after a possession of centuries. They were not grants out of public property: had these lands not been granted to the Church, they would have been granted to individuals or corporations like the rest.

Bishop Moriarty, in his statement of the Roman Catholics' claim to the Church property, expressly excepts all property acquired by the Church since the Reformation. It would be a strange sight to see the British Parliament setting at nought the grants of British sovereigns, and American republicans respecting them.

In fairness, too, I think no sufficient case can be made for depriving the Church of that proportion of the tithe rent charge that would fall to it, if the whole was divided *per capita* according to the religion of each, say the one-eighth.

Let it be remembered that this is a question of taking away from men that which they have had by law for three hundred years. Grant that the Church has no right to the whole, because seven-eighths of the people are not of her communion. On what principle of equity is she to be deprived of her fair proportion of the revenues? Surely, the landowners of the Church, who pay six-sevenths of the tithes, have at least a claim on that account not to be deprived of the proportion that the Church population justifies.

It may be answered that the majority of the people of Ireland, the Roman Catholics, do not desire their share of the rent charge, and therefore the Church shall not have her share. But this, if it was true, as it is not, is nothing else than the argument of the Dog in the manger. It may be reasonable for the Roman Catholics to refuse their own proportion, if they so please, but it is quite contrary to reason that they should thus deprive the Church of her proportion.

It is said, equality must be the rule.

When, however, the glebes and churches are left to the Church, and no glebes and churches provided for the Roman Catholics, is this equality? And when their life interests are preserved to the clergy of the Church, and no equivalent offered to the Roman Catholic clergy, though the money is actually there and it is a puzzle how to dispose of it, is that equality?

Plainly it is nothing of the sort. It is either equality so far as is consistent with equity to the Church—and that makes the true issue, not what is equal, but what is equitable ; in which case, whatever else is equitable has as good a claim to be left to the Church as the glebes and life interests—or else it is equality so far as is consistent with the views of a party and the interests of that party, which is no equality at all, but a sham.

I must not end without saying what, in my view, needs to be done by the Church itself to meet the difficulties, either of a compromise, or of still harder measure. Whether its revenues are largely reduced, or wholly taken away, there is no choice but that parishes must be grouped, otherwise the result will be, that whilst the richer parts of the country may provide themselves with religious ministrations, many large districts, and all the poorest, will be left wholly destitute.

The practical course would seem to be to occupy efficiently the centres of the Church population where we have considerable numbers, and group the outlying more thinly-peopled districts into large parishes, as large as the necessity arising from want of funds may compel. No doubt such parishes will often be too large, will require great activity, and after all will be inefficiently served. At worst, however, they will be better off than great colonial parishes. When complaints are made of the difficulty of working parishes 10 or 12 miles square, it is forgotten that colonial parishes are often many times larger.

In many cases, however, though it may be impossible to procure funds to enable such parishes to be subdivided, it may be possible to raise enough to pay a curate. Services will have to be held in different parts of such parishes on Sunday mornings, afternoons, and evenings, and weekday services on other evenings. Lay help must be resorted to, perhaps even on Sundays, in reading those parts of the service fit to be read by laymen, when the clergyman is engaged elsewhere; and thus these great parishes must be worked, till funds can be procured to subdivide them.

But it is essential that this grouping should be carried out at once. In order to carry it out, somebody must be authorised by Parliament, with power to make those arrangements that are needful for the purpose, otherwise there will be inextricable confusion between the present legal rights that will remain untouched and the new voluntary arrangements that are to take their place hereafter; as I have before shown, the life interests and rights of some of the clergy effectually stopping all new arrangements. There must be some power of dealing absolutely with these rights consistently with reasonable fairness to the present holders. Without power to that effect by Act of Parliament, a clergyman, even if consenting, could not be discharged from future duty in his parish. It is essential, too, that the Church should have the power of adding to the duty of those incumbents who remain, by enlarging their parishes, or removing them to other parishes with more duty. Surely it would be monstrous that clergymen with twenty or fifty parishioners should remain doing little or nothing, and with large incomes, whilst places numbering Church people by hundreds were without cure. A body of a few bishops and clergy, and as many laymen, with powers on the same principle as those of the English Universities Commission would probably be the best for the purpose. A large body could not do it.

There seems to be a general opinion that, provided the life interests of the present incumbents are left to them, the clergy will be no losers in a pecuniary sense by such a plan as that of last session. But this is a great mistake—a large number of the clergy will be great losers, especially the most able and vigorous class, by the almost entire stoppage of promotion to better livings. Mr. Gladstone saw this in the case of curates, and so was led to promise compensation to them. But the case of the incumbents of the smaller parishes is in reality much harder. Nearly all the patronage in the Irish Church being in the hands of the bishops, the result is a regular promotion step by step, of such of the clergy as have not some disqualification, from a curacy to a small living, then after eight or ten years to a better living, and at last to one still better. Of course, the smaller livings are most numerous, those under or about 200l.

a year. These are held by men of from thirty-five to forty-five years of age, and the loss to them by the stoppage of promotion, just at the time when their families are rising and so expenses increasing, will be most severe. It will be a great and direct pecuniary loss that will be felt in the very tenderest point, and that will leave them without prospect or even hope of bettering their condition afterwards in any way, or of educating and putting forward their children in their own condition of life, as but for the change they would have been able to do. The loss will really be much worse than if they were deprived of an appreciable part of their present incomes, and the prospect of future promotion was left. It would be more felt, because though the loss of present income might cause some straits, there would be hope for the future; whereas, in the other case, they will have no hope but to live and die in their present parishes in no better circumstances. All this portion of the Irish clergy, therefore, those of age and strength for work, would be equally well off with some present sacrifice, if arrangements could be made that would still carry on promotion.

It follows, too, that if parishes are grouped, many of the present clergy will not be wanted, and should be released from the obligation of further duty. Many of the older clergy, especially those unprepared for increased work, might reasonably be dealt with on the principle of superannuation. In many worldly services it is not thought unfair that men should be superannuated on a portion of their former emoluments free from further duty. A clergyman's income is not really net income; schools, charities, and other claims of a parish, and in case of ill-health a curate, absorb a considerable portion.

There are probably some of the clergy, both old and young, who would prefer to be discharged from future duty on equitable terms. Some would seek duty in England or the colonies, as curates and otherwise, and a sum of money in lieu of their life incomes would enable their claims in many cases to be compromised advantageously to the Church; the desire to advance children, and other pecuniary reasons, would lead to the same end with others. It is plain that the incumbent of a living of 200*l.* or 300*l.* a year, who gave up one-third of the income to be discharged from future duty, might by taking duty in England or the colonies even better his circumstances. To one with children of a suitable age, and wishing to go to the colonies, an equivalent in money for a portion of his income would enable him to put forward his children, whilst supporting himself by clerical duties there.

Now no less than 1,074 out of 1,518 incumbents of benefices have incomes under 300*l.* a year. It is plain, therefore, to how

·great an extent this course might be adopted without loss to any one. An incumbent with 300*l.* a year, giving up 100*l.* for an annuity of 200*l.* free from duty, and taking a curacy in England of 100*l.* a year *with chance of future promotion,* would be better off than remaining to live and die in his parish in Ireland without hope of promotion. In all livings below 300*l.* a year the gain to the Church would be greater in proportion as the living was smaller.

I am persuaded this course could be carried out to a large extent, if proper machinery for the purpose was provided. By a fitting appeal to the Bishops and Church in England and the Colonies, great aid would be surely procured in such a time of need, in the way of helping Irish clergymen at first to get nominations to curacies and small incumbencies.

But in justice to the laity and the whole Irish Church, such a course ought not to be made dependent on the likings of the clergy—a fair settlement of their present pecuniary claims is all they have a just right to. If a compromise for a part of their present incomes free from further duty will, by enabling them to take duty elsewhere, subject them to no loss, justice to others requires that such compromise, when for the good of the Church, should not be left merely at their pleasure, but should be made to depend on the decision of competent authority. * Many men would gladly make sacrifices for the love of their Church, especially it is to be hoped those having large Church incomes. Equivalent subscriptions from the laity would of course also be made. These would go much further by using them for life insurances. The circumstances of most of the landowners would make it easier for them to pay the premiums on insurances upon the lives of the incumbents of their parishes than to pay large sums at once to form an endowment fund. 50*l.* or 100*l.* a year could often be afforded, when 1,000*l.* or 2,000*l.* would be impracticable, while by allowing laymen to acquire the right of patronage in the new incumbencies in return for adequate contributions, some might be induced to help still more largely. Some may object to lay patronage, but a layman presenting to a parish endowed partly by himself is surely much less objectionable, than a parish depending on subscriptions, by the stoppage of which laymen could control the clergyman during his whole incumbency. Without power by Act of Parliament, neither insurances nor such lay patronage could be arranged.

An instance will best show how at worst such a plan could be worked out. The diocese of Cork, Cloyne, and Ross is coterminous with the county Cork, which is one-eighth of all Ireland ; the net income of its clergy is about 46,000*l.* per annum.

There are nearly 180 parishes, but only 90 Roman Catholic parishes.

If the Church parishes were grouped to form ninety new parishes, 23,000*l.* a year would give as sufficient incomes to ninety parishes as 46,000*l.* a year does to 180. In the west of the county most parishes have not less than 100 to 150 Church people; town parishes many more. Of the remote parishes that form the rocky headlands running out into the Atlantic, many are very poor, with large numbers of Church people, nearly all of the lower orders. Skull has 1,139; Kilmoe 590; Berehaven 313; Durrus 524. In these parishes there are hardly any gentry or persons in good circumstances. But in many of the Cloyne parishes, with the largest incomes, there are very few Protestants. These would be still more freely grouped. It is not too much to say that 20,000*l.* a year would suffice for this diocese.

If by arrangements with the clergy like those above suggested part of their present life incomes could be economised, say only 12,000*l.* per annum, this, at an average age of fifty-three, would insure about 230,000*l.*, which, at rather over 4 per cent. (the rate at which good security can be had in Ireland), would yield about 10,000*l.* per annum. It is probable more could be made thus, but this is taken as a minimum.

The Church could compromise the minor interests of parish clerks and expectations of curates on easier terms than the Government. The value of advowsons and glebes, subscriptions from the laity and arrangements allowing laymen to acquire rights of advowson, would go far to make up an income, not indeed sufficient, yet not wholly inadequate. I do not think it reasonable to expect that a full provision for the Irish Church should be made. There is not a full provision for the Church in England—witness London and the great towns. As much may rightly be left to private exertion in Ireland as now depends on it in England.

In the whole of Ireland, exclusive of the present three dioceses of Armagh, Down, and Dublin, there are only 283,000 members of the Church.

These are scattered over less than 1,100 ecclesiastical (not civil) parishes. If these parishes were grouped into 600, *i.e.*, with few exceptions grouped two into one, 283,000 souls would give an average of few more than 450 parishioners to each parish. But in not a few cases where Church people are very thin, three or four parishes might rightly be grouped into one; and in most town parishes and all parishes in cities the Church people are much more numerous, and count by hundreds and even thousands, and there are some country parishes with ex-

ceptionally large numbers. About one-sixth of these parishes
have thus over 500 Church people. As these are included in
the 283,000 souls, the average of country parishes after such
grouping would be less than 400 parishioners each, or eighty
families.

Now, are eighty families too many for one clergyman to
attend to, even though they may be scattered over a large area?
I think clearly not; and it is only the habits of the past state
of things that would make any difficulty in such cases. There
is a feeling in Ireland that a clergyman ought not to have hard
work, and has a right to complain if he has. The work that a
doctor or a lawyer does for the same income would be thought
too much for a clergyman. But this must be changed.

No doubt, if parishes are thus grouped, there will be cases in
which the area will be too large for efficient ministry. In
these the effort must be made to provide a curate. Probably
there will be a former glebe house and some land available for
him. Sometimes a landowner who is interested will provide a
salary or a large part of it. There will be Additional Curate
Societies to help. And where the case is really a strong one,
exertion will in time provide an endowment sufficient to enable
the parish to be divided.

Then as to bishoprics, good churchmen tell us we ought to
have plenty of bishops, more instead of fewer, and no doubt it
goes against one's Church feelings that bishoprics should be
suppressed. But in all Connaught there are no more than
about 40,000 Church people, and in the whole of Munster
80,000—numbers much less than those in either of the dioceses
of Armagh, Down, or Dublin. Common sense is forced to
acknowledge that either the one or the other number is not too
many for the oversight of one bishop. It will be said the areas
of such bishoprics will be large. But even now railroads are
so spread that a bishop could travel over every part of Munster
in less time and at less expense than he could have travelled
through the diocese of Cork twenty-five years ago, and every ten
years is sure to see these facilities extended.

Incomes on an average of 300l. a year each to 600 parishes
would amount to 180,000l. If 20,000l. a year more was
added for endowing the bishoprics, &c., it will be seen that all
Ireland, except Armagh, Down, and Dublin, would be not ill-
provided for on 200,000l. a year. These three dioceses are
much the most wealthy parts of Ireland, and therefore the best
able to help themselves; but add another 100,000l. a year for
them, and thus for 300,000l. a year, just half the present income
of the Irish Church, a not very insufficient provision would be
made for the future, and I suppose there are very few who

would grudge the Irish Church half its present income. If the boasted liberality in regard to money that it is meant to show on the treatment of the Church means anything at all, it can hardly mean less than this. As far as my knowledge of the country goes, the union of two parishes on an average into one with well-arranged boundaries, and the other suggestions I have made, could be carried out without injury to the Church.

I have made these statements, not as definite plans that can be carried out without many modifications, but as sketches to show in what direction our future arrangements necessarily lie. If we get the liberal treatment that has been promised, in any true sense, I think we have no reason to fear the result. It will, perhaps, be thought that some things I have stated may be taken advantage of by the opponents of the Church; but I have judged it better nevertheless openly to say them, as a fair compromise that will avoid the mischiefs of voluntaryism is all that I and many other laymen desire, and plain dealing will best approve itself to honest men.

In conclusion, I must express my conviction that peace ought to be the first, and second, and third object of every measure relating to Ireland, and that it is the indispensable condition of all improvement there. Protestant ascendancy is no doubt bad. But Roman Catholic ascendancy is no better. It is possible to promote ascendancy by other means than by Establishment and Endowment. If a great triumph is to be given to one side or the other, it is not in human nature that peace should be the result. The true mark to hit on all Irish questions, is that fair middle line that will remove all reasonable and honest grounds of offence without giving in to sentimental talk or jealous grudge, and that above all holds fast to sound principles.

If those honest principles that have been hitherto acted on by the British Parliament in all questions of pecuniary rights are now departed from in the manner of dealing with the Irish Church, instead of the settlement of the question being a step towards peace, it will be a step towards increased religious hatred and strife in Ireland. The furious ill-will and violence the elections have already produced both in North and South are surely warnings of the need of caution and moderation.

LISSELAN, *November* 21, 1868.

www.ingramcontent.com/pod-product-compliance
Lightning Source LLC
Chambersburg PA
CBHW021558270326
41931CB00009B/1282